What is a Grassland?

Grasslands are environments in which grass is the main plant, rather than shrubs or trees.

Grasslands need 25 to 100 centimetres of rain each year. If they get less than this, they turn into deserts. If grasslands get much more rain, lots of trees grow and they become forests.

There are two main types of grassland – **savannas** (also called tropical grasslands) and temperate grasslands.

Savannas are found in warm **climates** that have wet and dry seasons.

Temperate grasslands have cold winters and warm summers with some rain. Temperate grasslands are also called **steppes** or **prairies**.

Fires are common during a dry season. They can be caused by lightning strikes

Some grassland animals jump to get above the tall grass.

GO FACT!
DID YOU KNOW?
African savannas get three times more rain than Australian savannas.

Some grassland birds, like this ostrich, do not need trees to make a nest.

Savannas and temperate grasslands have different types of soil and numbers of trees.

Savannas have thin, **porous** soil. This means that water drains through it very quickly. The soil does not have many **nutrients** from rotting plants and animal droppings. Trees and shrubs are dotted across the savanna.

Temperate grasslands have deep, dark soil. The soil is held together by rotting grass roots. The roots provide lots of nutrients for the soil. Because of the nutrients, people use temperate grasslands to grow crops and graze animals.

There are almost no trees or large shrubs in temperate grasslands. It is too cold and dry for them to grow.

North American prairies are mainly used for growing crops.

African elephants create grasslands by knocking down trees.

Spinifex grasses grow in sandy soil. They cover about 20 per cent of Australia.

Some grasslands are covered with water for short periods.

Grasslands of the World

About 40 per cent of the Earth's land is grassland.

Grasslands are found on every continent except Antarctica. Their names depend on the language of the country they are in.

A grassland in Peru.

Grasslands of the World

NORTH AMERICA

Los Llanos

GO FACTS

THE LARGEST

The five countries with the largest grassland areas are Australia, Russia, China, Canada and the USA.

In South America, the Los Llanos grassland is the size of France. Los Llanos means "the flat plains" in Spanish. In southern Africa, the temperate grasslands are known as veldts, which means "fields" and in central Africa, the Serengeti means "endless plains". The huge grassland in Hungary is called the Puszta, which means "barren plain". The Kakadu National Park in Australia takes its name from an Aboriginal language spoken in that area.

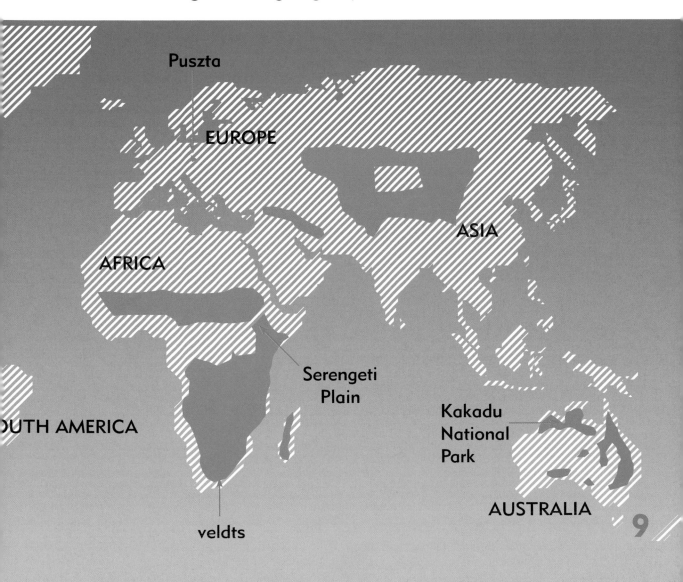

Puszta

EUROPE

ASIA

AFRICA

SOUTH AMERICA

Serengeti Plain

Kakadu National Park

veldts

AUSTRALIA

 # The Mongolian Steppes

The Mongolian steppes are dry temperate grasslands in Central Asia.

Temperatures on the steppes vary widely. It can be as hot as 30 °C (86 °F) in summer and as cold as −30 °C (-22 °F) in winter.

Nomads look after camels, sheep, goats and cows in the Mongolian steppes. They travel great distances every year with their herds.

The steppes are also home to many wild animals. There are eagles, foxes, hares and cranes.

Golden eagle

A rare steppe animal is the Przewalski horse. This **species** of horse almost became **extinct** when people hunted them for food. The last 31 Przewalski horses in the world lived in zoos. In 1992, a small group of horses was released back into the wilds of the Mongolian steppes.

The Bactrian camel is used for wool, milk, meat and leather. It has two humps.

DID YOU KNOW?
A camel's hump stores fat, not water. The fat is an energy source. If the fat is not replaced, the hump shrinks and droops.

The steppes cover about 20 per cent of Mongolia's land.

The Przewalski horse is the national symbol of Mongolia.

Grassland Plants

Grasses are not the only plants in grasslands. Forbs and sedges grow there, as well as trees and shrubs.

There are about 7500 species of grass. They can survive the harsh climate of a grassland. They store food in their roots to stay alive during the long dry seasons. Grasses have thin leaves so they don't lose too much water. They have deep roots to help stop the plants being pulled up by animals.

Forbs are non-woody flowering plants. Wildflowers and herbs are forbs. Shrubs and trees are woody flowering plants.

Sedges are grass-like plants that grow in fresh water. Papyrus and bulrushes are types of sedges.

A seed pod from a baobab tree

12

Baobab trees store thousands of litres of water in their trunks.

GO FACTS

THE TALLEST

Elephant grass is the tallest grass in the world. It can grow four metres high.

Giraffes can reach the highest branches of acacia trees in Africa.

13

How Grass Gets Water

Some plants have one, long, main root called a tap root. Most grasses have lots of small roots. What type of root is the best for getting water?

You will need:

- two pieces of cotton rope (about ten centimetres long)
- two small glass jars
- water

Directions:

1. Unravel the end of one piece of rope. Make half of it into loose threads. It now looks like grass roots.

2. Put half a cup of water into each jar. Place the piece of rope with loose ends into one jar. Count to 20 and then remove it.

3. Place the other piece of rope into the other jar. Count to 20 and then remove it.

1

2

3

Measure the amount of water left in each jar.

Lots of thin threads soak up more than one thick rope. This is the way grasses absorb water.

15

Grassland Animals

Grasslands are home to many different animal species.

African grasslands hold the biggest herds and greatest variety of hoofed mammals on Earth. They hold 72 of the world's 84 species of antelopes, including eland, impalas, gazelles, oryx and kudu.

Up to 16 grazing species may share the same area. They eat different parts of the grass plant, encouraging the plant to regrow. In African savannas, zebras eat the toughest and longest parts of the grass. Antelopes follow the zebras and eat the grass shoots. Animal droppings help to **fertilise** the soil.

Termite mounds up to four metres tall are common in the savannas of Australia and Africa. In Mongolia, eagles nest on the ground because there are no trees.

Dung beetles eat animal droppings.

16

Kangaroos are common in Australian grasslands.

American bison have excellent hearing and smell, but poor eyesight.

GO FACT!

THE FASTEST

Cheetahs are the fastest land animal in the world. They can sprint at 114 kilometres per hour.

Savanna Seasons

The African savanna has cycles of dry and wet seasons.

1 Dry season

Hot winds begin to blow. Grasses die off at the surface, but the roots remain alive. Fires may burn whole areas. Waterholes dry up, forcing many animals to **migrate**. There are often violent thunderstorms before the wet season starts.

2 Wet season

When the rains start, grass can grow 2.5 centimetres in one day. Rivers run again and waterholes refill. Many animals give birth because there is plenty of food. The rain may last for months or only weeks.

3 Return to dry season

The grassland begins to dry out again after the rains stop. The grass is eaten or dies back at the surface. It will grow again when the rains return.

Animals on the Move

Millions of animals migrate across the grasslands of Africa's Serengeti Plain. Migrate means to move to another place.

Wildebeests are a type of antelope that migrate. Each year, more than one million wildebeests migrate 2000 kilometres. They travel to find the fresh grass that grows after the rains. Thousands of zebras and gazelles migrate with them.

When the grasslands dry out, the animals move, travelling 50 to 80 kilometres each day. The wildebeests spend months in the north of the Serengeti. They then follow the rains south, back to where their journey began.

Many wildebeests die during the journey. Before the migration begins again, the wildebeests give birth to calves.

The animals must cross the deep Masai Mara River.

18

The herds stay near waterholes during the dry season.

Lions, hyenas and crocodiles hunt the migrating animals.

Wildebeests can sense where the rains are falling.

GO FACT!

THE LONGEST

The longest animal migration in the world is by the sooty shearwater, a seabird. It flies about 74 000 kilometres around the Pacific Ocean each year.

Does It Migrate?

Grassland animal	Is it a plant eater?	Does it migrate?	
Wildebeest	yes	yes	
Zebra	yes	yes	
Rhinoceros	yes	no	
Giraffe	yes	no	
Hyena	no	no	
Cheetah	no	no	

Glossary

climate   the usual weather conditions in a particular place

extinct   no longer existing; died out

fertilise   to spread something on soil or plants that helps plants grow

migrate   to move from one area to another, usually to find food

nomad   a person who moves from place to place

nutrient   anything that plants or animals use to live and grow

porous   allows liquid or air to pass through

prairie   a name for a temperate grassland

savanna   a name for a tropical grassland

species   a set of animals or plants in which the members look the same

steppe   a name for a temperate grassland in Central Asia

Index